The Mommy Button

An Answer to a Curious Child's Question

Authored By:
BethAnn Salinas

Edited By:
Natalie Hansen

Illustrated By:
Gail Hansen

CrossBooks™
A Division of LifeWay
One LifeWay Plaza
Nashville, TN 37234
www.crossbooks.com
Phone: 1-866-768-9010

Scripture taken from the King James Version of the Bible.

First published by CrossBooks 09/02/2014

ISBN: 978-1-4627-3907-3 (sc)
ISBN: 978-1-4627-3906-6 (e)

Printed in the United States of America.

This book is printed on acid-free paper.

CROSSBOOKS

Acknowledgement Page

I am thankful God created me and loves me as one of His precious children. I am also thankful to God for sending His Son Jesus into my life as He has won for me salvation in heaven through His death and resurrection! I am grateful for receiving the gift of the Holy Spirit at my Baptism where I was called to be a child of God's eternal family. Oh, The Blessed Trinity! "For you formed my inward parts; you knitted me together in my mother's womb" (Psalm 139:13).

I would like to acknowledge my children, especially my first-born child who inspired the idea of a physical connection with me. I love my children dearly as they are precious gifts from God. I love you Sunshine and Duck Guy!

I really appreciate all the time and effort my editor, Natalie Hansen, took to work on this book. She is a wonderful friend and great editor.

I am especially grateful and lovingly thankful to my sister, Gail Hansen, for illustrating this book. She is a great sister and friend to me.

I extend my love and thankfulness to my mom and dad for encouraging me and always praying for me. I also thank them for sharing their faith by taking me to church and supporting my needs.

I thank God daily for my husband, Adam Salinas, my spiritual support throughout this process and every day of our lives together. I am blessed by God to have a loving and caring husband who encouraged me to write this book.

Additionally, I am truly thankful for all the support and care my friend Debbie Waltz has given me. She taught me that regardless of the limitations you have in life God will use you as His instrument!

<u>For a Child or Children</u>:

Dear Heavenly Father,

Thank you for creating me. You took care of me through my mommy button! I appreciate that you gave me

mommy and daddy. You gave me life, and give me eternal life in heaven through your Son, Jesus Christ.

In His name, I pray. Amen!

For Moms:

Abba Father,

Please help me take care of this precious gift from you. Give
me strength to help him or her grow physically,

mentally, and most of all, provide this child with a strong faith
in Jesus (place hand on your womb as a blessing).

May His face shine upon you, be gracious unto you, and
grant you peace (Numbers 6:25-26). Amen!

For Siblings:

Dear God,

Grant me the patience to wait for my new brother or sister to
grow, and bless them during this time. Help them

breathe and eat through their mommy button. Protect and guard them
from danger. Thank you for giving me a chance to be a big brother or sister,
and help me teach this new sibling about you, our Savior, Jesus.

In His Holy Name, I pray. Amen!

For Adopted Children:

Dear Gracious Father,

Thank you for taking care of my biological mother. I am thankful
that my mother took care of me in her womb.

You created and sustained me. I am very thankful that you gave me a family,
especially my mommy! I know we will always be connected.
In Jesus Name, I pray. Amen!

One day a little girl was looking at her belly, and poking at her belly button. She asked her caregiver, "What is this on my tummy?" "That's your belly button sweetie." "Oh!" she said. "It doesn't look like a button."

2

Later that evening at home, the little girl went to her Daddy and asked, "Do you have a belly button, Daddy?" "I sure do, honey."

3

"Poke mine," replied her Daddy. "Woo, Woo." "Why did you make such a noise?" asked the little girl. "It is my sound button!" "Your sound button?" she questioned.

4

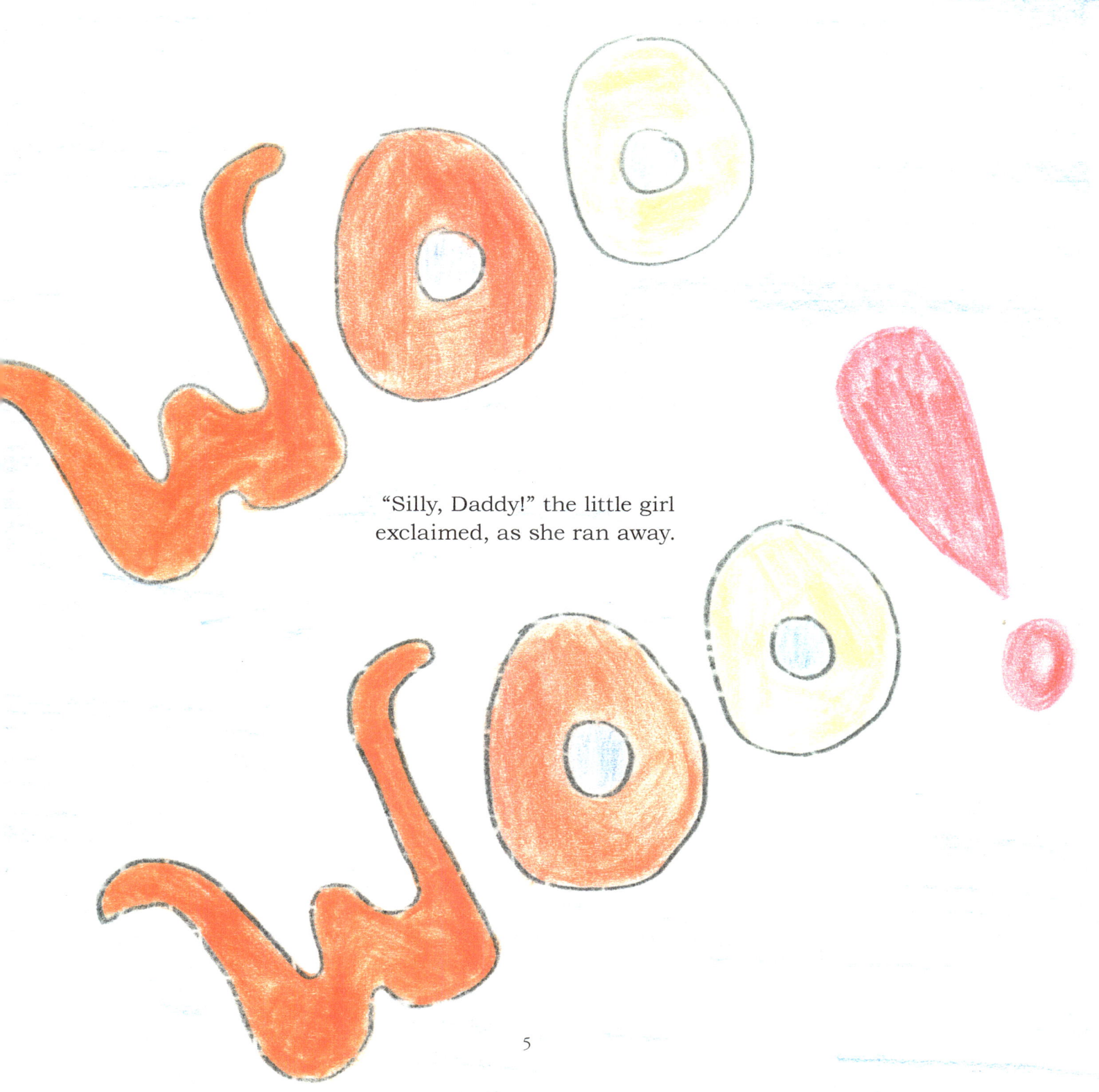

"Silly, Daddy!" the little girl exclaimed, as she ran away.

5

Since the little girl liked clear answers, she decided to ask her Granny the question. "Why such a long face, my dear?"

"Well, I keep asking people about this..." replied the little girl, as she pointed to her belly button. "Why, that is your navel!" responded her Grandma. "A navel is something you are born with. Remember to wash it, and keep it clean."

7

At bath time, the little girl's Mother said, "I heard you have been asking others about your belly button."

"Yes, Mommy, I want to know its name. Everyone calls it something different," replied the little girl.

Her Mommy laughed, as she smiled at her curious child. "Well, what have you learned?" With a confused look on her face, the little girl answered, "Miss Jen said it was my belly button... Daddy said it was a noise button... and Granny said it was my navel, and that I needed to keep it clean."

"Oh!" Mommy said. "Well actually, it is your Mommy button!"
"My Mommy button?" asked the little girl.

10

"Yes," Mommy replied, "God knitted you inside my womb so tenderly, that He made a cord which attached you to me. When you were growing inside me that is how you ate and got oxygen to breathe.

Then, when you were born, the cord fell off and you were left with a Mommy button."

The little girl's face lit up with delight because she finally got her answer. "So Mommy, you mean we are connected forever?" Her Mother smiled. "Why, yes indeed – forever and ever!"

CPSIA information can be obtained at www.ICGtesting.com
Printed in the USA
LVOW01s1729161014

409076LV00001B/1/P